Employee's Survival Guide to Change

Prosci Change Management Series

Employee's Survival Guide to Change: Hiatt, Jeffrey M.
Editor: Hooks, Jennifer L.
Illustrations: Turley, Joyce M.

ISBN 1-930885-17-2
Library of Congress Control Number: 2001132449

Employee's Survival Guide to Change © 2001 Prosci Research
Illustrations © 2001 Joyce M. Turley, Dixon Cove Design
Cover Design © 2001 Joyce M. Turley, Dixon Cove Design

Revised edition © 2002 Prosci Research

Learning Center Publications

Contents

Introduction

Change can happen at any time to anyone. When change happens to someone else, it can be fascinating to talk about. However, when change happens to you, it can be worrisome and uncomfortable. You may be uncertain about what lies ahead. You may have concerns about job security, finances or learning new skills.

Most employees who find themselves the targets of change experience these same feelings. What employees don't know is that they play a key role in the success of change. More importantly, the more informed you are, the more likely you will survive the change and advance professionally in a changing environment.

So, what does it take to be a survivor in today's rapidly changing companies?

1. A solid understanding of the change process and your role in it.

2. Answers to questions that will help you succeed.

3. A set of tools to help you manage change and reach the outcome you want.

As an employee facing the uncertainty of change, one of the most important things you can do is to take time to read this guidebook. Wisdom resulting from research with more than 700 organizations over four years waits for you in the following pages. The key to professional and personal success during change is in your hands!

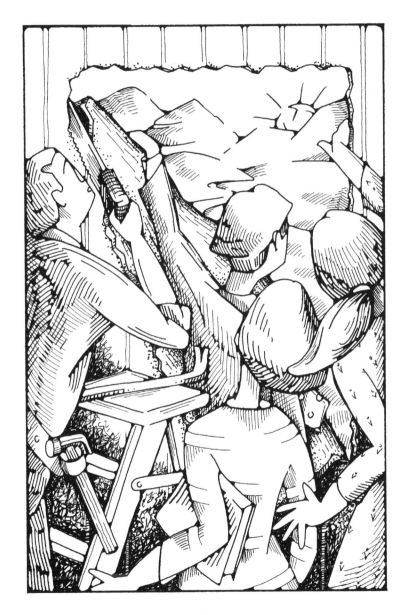

Part 1:
Frequently Asked Questions
(FAQs) About Change

Why is change happening now?

You may feel like change is happening all of a sudden and that it is directed right at you. In reality, most changes begin outside the company many months or even years before internal change takes place. Research shows that most major business changes are a response to changes in the external marketplace.

These external marketplace changes can result in:

- Loss of market share (your company is losing money).

- New offers or capabilities by competitors (they're creating new business faster than your company).

- Lower prices (their cost of doing business is lower, resulting in better prices to their customers).

External business drivers take time to set in. If they have already affected the bottom line of your company, change is needed immediately. In some cases it is already too late — the internal change should have started much sooner.

What is the risk of not changing?

When external marketplace changes become apparent inside the organization, managers suddenly realize the risks of not changing.

For businesses, the risk of not changing could mean:

- Loss of jobs (even at the executive level).

- Failure in the marketplace.

- Bankruptcy or loss of revenue.

For employees, the risk of not changing could mean:

- Job dissatisfaction.

- Fewer promotional opportunities.

- Lower job security in the long term.

- Immediate loss of employment.

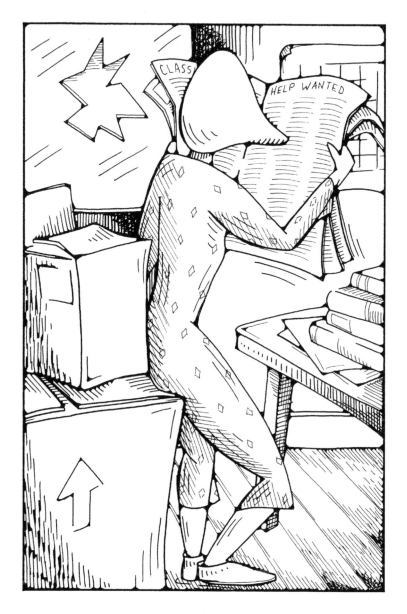

What is the rush?

Employees usually find out what is happening after the fact. Organizations do not always share financial information or talk about poor performance issues with employees. Therefore, when change is needed quickly, employees may be taken by surprise.

On one hand, organizations are trying to implement change as quickly as possible, while on the other hand, employees are one step behind trying to understand why the change is needed and how they will be impacted.

Unfortunately for the company, most employees are in no hurry to change. In fact, many employees may not see the need to change at all. Forcing employees to change when they do not understand the business reasons can be a lot like pushing a giant cube of Jello — you might have an impact, but no real overall shift occurs.

When the force is removed, everything returns to the way it was before.

If I wait long enough, will the change just go away?

If financial success of the organization depends on change, then you can expect the change to happen with or without you. Waiting will usually not change the outcome.

In most cases a company will change — even in the face of resistance from employees — especially if financial success is at stake.

This does not imply that change will be bad for you. In the end many changes result in positive outcomes for employees. Benefits might include better tools, improved work processes, more secure jobs and new opportunities for you to advance your career.

What will change mean to me?

Change to a business can include:

- New ways of doing work.
- New systems or tools.
- New reporting structures.
- New job roles.
- New products or services.
- New markets or geographic locations.

How will the change impact me?

That depends on your current job, the extent of the change, and the choices you make in response to the change.

With small changes, you may not be impacted at all. With major changes, you may be doing new work, using new tools or reporting to a new manager. With radical changes to the business, some employees may work in other departments or even move to other companies.

When the change is implemented, each person will be affected differently. In the end, how you react to the change plays an important role in how the change will impact you.

The good news is:

The actual impact of the change on you is directly related to how you react to the change.

In other words, you are in control of how you respond to change. Better yet, how the organization views you and your future role in the company may depend on your response to change and the choices you make.

What are my choices?

Your choices about how to respond to change will vary as the organization moves through the change process. Think about the change in these time periods:

> **When the change is first announced,** but before the change is implemented.

> **During the change process:** when the new solution is being deployed.

> **After the change is in place:** following the implementation of the solution.

Your choices and their consequences depend on which phase your organization is in. The following pages provide potential choices you may make and the likely outcome of those choices.

In some cases choices you make may have negative outcomes. They may be bad for you and for the organization. Other choices you make will benefit you and enhance your ability to thrive in a changing organization.

The choices shown on the following pages are separated into:

- Choices with typically **negative** outcomes.
- Choices with typically **positive** outcomes.

These examples help illustrate the conscious and unconscious decisions we all make regarding change.

Before the change	Choices that typically have a negative outcome

1. Talk badly about the proposed change with your peers or subordinates.

2. Talk negatively about the organization or people in the organization.

3. Talk one way in public, but say otherwise in private conversations.

4. Stop performing your current responsibilities or perform them carelessly.

5. Have secret meetings with your subordinates where the change is minimized or not taken seriously.

Before the change

Choices that typically have a positive outcome

1. Learn about the change.

2. Ask how you can help.

3. Find out how you can prepare for the change.

4. Display a positive outlook.

5. Encourage constructive conversations with fellow employees.

6. Be open and honest with your feedback about the change.

7. Be quiet and curious. (This choice is acceptable during the early phases of a change.)

| During the change | Choices that typically have a negative outcome |

1. Block progress or sabotage the change process.

2. Talk negatively about the change in private conversations.

3. Ignore the change — pretend that it is not happening (denial).

4. Prevent others from participating in the design of the solution or implementation of the design.

During the change

Choices that typically have a positive outcome

1. Ask questions about the future.

2. Ask how the change will impact day-to-day operations.

3. Provide input to the solution.

4. Find out what new skills and abilities you will need to perform effectively after the change is in place.

5. Assess your own strengths and weaknesses.

6. Identify training that will be available to fill skill gaps.

7. Take advantage of the change to develop new skills and grow professionally.

After the change	Choices that typically have a negative outcome

1. Avoid using the new work processes or tools whenever possible.

2. Tell peers or subordinates that using the new work processes or tools is not a big deal and shouldn't be taken too seriously.

3. Talk negatively about the organization with customers.

4. Revert to the old way of doing work when problems or issues arise with the change.

5. Take advantage of problems during implementation to argue why the change will never work.

| After the change | Choices that typically have a positive outcome |

1. Reinforce the change with peers and subordinates.

2. Help the business achieve the objectives of the change (be results-oriented).

3. Avoid reverting back to old processes or ways of doing work when problems arise with the new processes and systems.

4. Help solve problems that arise with new work processes and tools.

What are the consequences of not changing?

The consequences to you of not changing depend on how critical the change is to the business.

For changes that are less critical to business success, the consequences may be minimal. However, if you elect not to support the change, and the change is critical to the success of the organization, the likely consequences are:

1. Loss of employment.

2. Reassignment or transfer with the potential for lower pay.

3. Lost opportunities for promotion or advancement in the organization.

4. Reduced job satisfaction as you fight the organization and the organization fights you.

What are the benefits of supporting the change?

The benefits of supporting the change, especially changes that are critical to the success of the organization, include:

1. Enhanced respect and reputation within the organization.

2. Improved growth opportunities (especially for active supporters of the change).

3. Increased job satisfaction (knowing you are helping your organization respond effectively to a rapidly changing marketplace).

4. Improved job security.

Other FAQs

What if I disagree with the change? What if I feel they are fixing the wrong problem?

Be patient. Keep an open mind. Make sure you understand the business reasons for the change. However, don't be afraid to voice your specific objections or concerns. If your objections are valid, chances are good they will come to light and be resolved. If you feel strongly against a specific element of the change, let the right people know and do it in an appropriate manner.

What if they've tried before and failed?

The history of your company may include some previous change projects that failed. If failure is what employees are accustomed to, the organization will have a hard time erasing the past. In order for companies to be successful, everyone must be prepared to accept the past as history and focus on what lies ahead.

What if I am forced to do more for the same pay?

When your organization is undergoing a change, this usually means that new processes, systems or skills are required. Your role in the changed environment may include learning these new processes or acquiring new skills. Indeed, some of your responsibilities may change.

For the old way of doing things, compensation may actually decrease as the value of that work to the organization goes down. However, compensation for new work may increase as the value for new services and products increases. This is a part of change.

Part 2:
Taking Control of Change

The ADKAR model

The ADKAR[1] model is a powerful tool to help you answer the question:

"How can I stay in control (both personally and professionally) of the change process?"

Research in change management and business process design with more than 700 companies over four years shows that successful change can be modeled and repeated. By using this model you can:

- determine where you are in the change process.
- create a successful action plan for personal and professional advancement.

---

1. The ADKAR model is a registered trademark of Prosci Research.

The ADKAR model has five elements:

- **Awareness** of the need for change.

- **Desire** to make the change happen.

- **Knowledge** about how to change.

- **Ability** to implement new skills and behaviors.

- **Reinforcement** to retain the change once it has been made.

Before you assess where you are in the change process, take a minute to look at the model more closely. In the following examples, we look at a simple work scenario and two personal case studies.

After reviewing these examples, complete the worksheets for both a personal change you are going through and for the business change you are experiencing.

What you will discover is that this simple model allows you to break down a change into parts, understand where the change is failing and address that impact point. This type of intervention results in energy directed at the most critical component of change.

A first look at the model:
A work scenario

If you are an employee in an organization undergoing change, your reaction to the change and how you are viewed by the organization will be directly affected by each of the five elements in the ADKAR model.

Take for example the implementation of a new software tool. If the change is implemented and you believe it was not needed (i.e., you were not **aware** that any changes were required), then your reaction might be:

"This is a waste of time."

"Why change if it was working just fine before?"

"If it ain't broke, don't fix it."

"They never tell us what's going on!"

Our natural reaction to change, even in the best circumstances, is to resist. **Awareness** of the business need to change is a critical ingredient of any change and must come first.

36

If someone had taken the time to explain that the old software would no longer be supported by the vendor, and that new software was necessary to meet the needs of your customers, then your reaction (based on this **awareness**) would likely be very different:

"How soon will this happen?"

"How will this impact me?"

"Will I receive new training?"

Take this same example one step further. Assume you were made **aware** that a change was required, but you had no **desire** to participate or support the change.

Now the tables are turned, and you will become the target of an emotional response from individuals within the organization. You may be labeled as difficult, inflexible or unsupportive. Some may say you lack initiative or vision. You may be called a cynic or pessimist.

Awareness and desire are two critical components of the change model. In the personal examples that follow, you will see how the other elements of the model play a role in a successful change.

Examples from personal experience

Changing a child's behavior

Changing unwanted behavior in children follows the ADKAR model well. Children first need to know what they are doing is wrong. This **awareness** often comes when an upset parent tells the child he is doing something wrong. Simply knowing it is wrong, however, will not stop most children. Their natural inclination is to test the boundaries and push the limits.

Consequences, either positive or negative, are usually required. These consequences impact the child's **desire** to change. However, the process cannot stop here. Given proper motivation to change, children need a role model to understand what the proper behavior looks like. They need examples to give them the **knowledge** of what the correct behavior is.

Next, they need practice. Few children can change immediately; it is an ongoing process requiring them to develop new skills and habits. They need time to develop the **ability** to act in a new way.

Finally, they need **reinforcement** to keep the good behavior going. This may be in the form of positive encouragement or other types of rewards.

Coaching a sport

In this case study example, a parent was attempting to improve the batting style and skill of his son playing baseball. Dad was concerned that his son's batting was not up to the level of the other boys on the team. He searched the Internet for batting videos and purchased a tape for his son. For weeks he tried to get his son to watch the video on batting mechanics. With some parental persuasion, Dad was able to get his son to watch part of the tape. After that, the video was left untouched.

The father's attempt to educate his son failed and resulted only in a frustrated parent. He finally sat down with his son and asked him why he would not watch the tape and use it to improve his batting. His son replied that he just enjoyed playing baseball with his friends, and it did not matter to him if his batting was as good as some of the other boys.

In this example the father skipped steps in the ADKAR model (from **awareness** to **knowledge**). His son had no **desire** to change and was content just to be out there playing the game. Dad's efforts to build **knowledge** failed because his son lacked the **desire** to change.

The ADKAR model creates focus on the first element that is the root cause of failure. When you approach change using this model, you can immediately identify where the process is breaking down and which elements are being overlooked. This avoids generic conversations about the change that rarely produce actionable steps.

ADKAR can help you plan effectively for a new change or diagnose why a current change is failing. In some cases, corrective action can be taken and the change successfully implemented. Here are the five steps again.

- **Awareness** of the need for change.

- **Desire** to make the change happen.

- **Knowledge** about how to change.

- **Ability** to implement new skills and behaviors.

- **Reinforcement** to retain the change once it has been made.

Now it's your turn.

The best way to understand the usefulness of this type of model for business change management is to apply the model to a personal situation. Using a situation you are close to will help separate the key elements of the ADKAR model.

Worksheets have been provided on the following pages that will guide you through the application of the model. Begin by identifying a change you are having difficulty making in another person (a friend, family member or work associate). Complete the worksheets to the best of your ability, rating each area on a scale of 0% to 100%.

Be sure you select a change you have been trying to make happen in a friend, colleague or family member that is not working regardless of your continued efforts.

Introduction

Briefly describe the **personal** change you are trying to implement with a friend, family member or work associate.

_____

_____

_____

_____

_____

_____

_____

_____

_____

_____

_____

_____

_____

_____

_____

_____

_____

_____

_____

_____

_____

_____

_____

1. List the reasons you believe the change is necessary.

_____

_____

_____

_____

_____

_____

_____

_____

_____

_____

_____

_____

_____

_____

_____

_____

Review these reasons and ask yourself the degree to which the person you are trying to change is aware of these reasons.

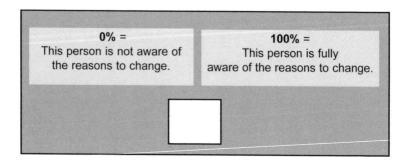

0% =	**100% =**
This person is not aware of the reasons to change.	This person is fully aware of the reasons to change.

2. List the factors or consequences (good and bad) for this person that create a *desire* to change.

_____

_____

_____

_____

_____

_____

_____

_____

_____

_____

_____

_____

_____

_____

_____

_____

_____

Consider these motivating factors, including the person's conviction in these factors and the associated consequences. Assess his/her desire to change.

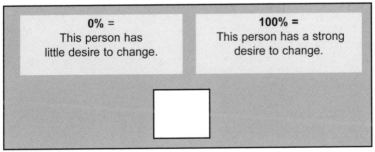

0% = This person has little desire to change.	100% = This person has a strong desire to change.

3. List the skills and *knowledge* needed for the change.

_____

_____

_____

_____

_____

_____

_____

_____

_____

_____

_____

_____

_____

_____

Rate this person's knowledge or training in these areas. (0% - 100%)?

0% = This person does not have training or the required knowledge to implement the change.	**100% =** This person has the training and knowledge to implement the change.

4. Considering the skills and knowledge identified in Step 3, evaluate the person's ability to perform these skills or act on this knowledge.

_____

_____

_____

_____

_____

_____

_____

_____

_____

_____

_____

_____

_____

_____

_____

_____

_____

To what percent do you rate this person's *ability* to implement the new skills, knowledge and behaviors to support the change (0% - 100%)?

0% = This person has not yet developed the skills and behaviors to support the change.	100% = This person has mastered the skills and behaviors to support the change.

5. List the *reinforcements* that will help to retain the change. Are incentives in place to reinforce the change and make it stick?

_____

_____

_____

_____

_____

_____

_____

_____

_____

_____

_____

_____

_____

_____

_____

_____

_____

To what percent do you rate the *reinforcements* as helping support the change (0% - 100%)?

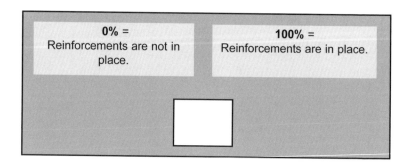

0% = Reinforcements are not in place.	100% = Reinforcements are in place.

Now transfer your scores from each worksheet to the table shown in Figure 1. Take a moment to review your scores. Highlight those areas that scored a 50% or below, and identify (using the order listed on the scoresheet) which was the first area to score less than 50%. Note that in the example worksheet in Figure 2, **desire** was the first area in this example to score less than 50%.

Brief description of the change: _____	Percent true or complete
1. *Awareness* of the need to change? Notes:_____	
2. *Desire* to make the change happen? Notes:_____	
3. *Knowledge* about how to change? Notes:_____	
4. *Ability* to change? Notes:_____	
5. *Reinforcement* to retain the change? Notes:_____	

Figure 1 - Change evaluation worksheet

Brief description of the change:	Percent true or complete
1. *Awareness* of the need to change? Notes:_____	*75%*
2. *Desire* to make the change happen? Notes:_____	*20%*
3. *Knowledge* about how to change? Notes:_____	*75%*
4. *Ability* to change? Notes:_____	*100%*
5. *Reinforcement* to retain the change? Notes:_____	*80%*

Figure 2 - Sample evaluation worksheet

Notes

_____

_____

_____

_____

_____

_____

_____

_____

_____

_____

_____

_____

_____

_____

_____

_____

_____

_____

_____

_____

_____

_____

_____

_____

Now consider the first area in which your score was 50% or below. You must address this area before anything else is done. For example, if you identified **awareness** as the area with a low score, then working on desire, knowledge or skill development will not help you make the change happen.

On the other hand, if you identified **desire**, then continually repeating your reasons for change is not adequate to move this person forward. Once they know these reasons, you must address their inherent desire to change. Desire may stem from negative or positive consequences. The negative consequences have to be great enough to overcome their personal threshold to resist change (same for the positive consequences).

If **knowledge** was the area you identified, then you want to be careful not to dwell on the reasons for change and the motivating factors. This could be discouraging for someone already at this phase. What is needed is education and training for the skills and behaviors that are needed for change.

If **ability** was the area selected with the low score, then two elements are required to move forward.

- The person will need time to develop the new skills and behaviors. Just like learning a new sport or any new skill, time is required to develop new abilities.

- The person will need ongoing coaching and support. No one-time training event or educational program will substitute for ongoing coaching and mentoring.

Finally, if **reinforcement** was the area identified, then you will need to investigate if necessary elements are present to keep the person from reverting to old behaviors. Address the incentives or consequences for not continuing to act in the new way.

Now that you have completed the ADKAR model for a personal change, you can follow the same process for the change happening at work. This process should give you insight as to where you are in the change process, and what steps you can take to not only survive change, but advance professionally in a changing business environment.

Business change

Briefly describe the change that is being implemented at your company.

_____

_____

_____

_____

_____

_____

_____

_____

_____

_____

_____

_____

_____

_____

_____

_____

_____

_____

_____

_____

_____

_____

1. Describe your *awareness* of the need to change. What are the business, customer or competitor issues that have created a need to change?

_____

_____

_____

_____

_____

_____

_____

_____

_____

_____

_____

_____

_____

_____

_____

_____

To what percent do you rate your *awareness* of the need to change (0%-100%)?

0% =	100% =
I am not aware of the business reasons to change.	I am fully aware of the business reasons to change.

2. List the factors or consequences (good and bad) related to this change that affect your *desire* to change.

_____

_____

_____

_____

_____

_____

_____

_____

_____

_____

_____

_____

_____

_____

_____

_____

_____

Consider these motivating factors, including your conviction in these factors and the associated consequences. Assess your overall desire to change.

0% = I have little desire to change.	**100% =** I have a strong desire to change.

3. List the skills and knowledge needed to support this change.

_____

_____

_____

_____

_____

_____

_____

_____

_____

_____

_____

_____

_____

_____

Do you have a clear understanding of the change and the skills you will need to operate in the new environment? Have you received education or training to learn these skills? To what percent do you rate your *knowledge* of the change (0% - 100%)?

0% =	100% =
I do not have training or the required knowledge to implement the change.	I have training and the required knowledge to implement the change.

4. Considering the skills and knowledge identified in Step 3, assess your overall proficiency in each area (low, medium, high).

_____

_____

_____

_____

_____

_____

_____

_____

_____

_____

_____

_____

_____

_____

_____

_____

_____

_____

Review your evaluations and rate your overall *ability* to change (0% - 100%).

0% =	**100%=**
I have not yet developed the skills and behaviors to support the change.	I have mastered the skills and behaviors to support the change.

5. List the *reinforcements* that will help retain the change. Are incentives in place to reinforce the change and make it stick?

_____

_____

_____

_____

_____

_____

_____

_____

_____

_____

_____

_____

_____

_____

_____

_____

To what percent do you rate the *reinforcements* as adequate to sustain the change (0% - 100%)?

0%=	100% =
No reinforcements are in place.	Sufficient reinforcements are in place.

Transfer your scores from the worksheets to the table below. Circle the first area where you scored 50% or less.

Brief description of the change:	Percent true or complete
1. *Awareness* of the need to change? Notes:_____	
2. *Desire* to make the change happen? Notes:_____	
3. *Knowledge* about how to change? Notes:_____	
4. *Ability* to change? Notes:_____	
5. *Reinforcement* to retain the change? Notes:_____	

Based on your scores in this exercise, you can take specific steps to overcome the barriers to change. These steps are described on the following pages.

For example, let's assume you scored the **awareness** question at 20%, meaning you know a little about the change, but not enough to be completely aware of why it is happening and the associated business reasons driving it. You would then follow the directions in Step 1. If you scored above 50% on awareness but low on **desire**, then move directly to Step 2, and so on.

Step 1: Awareness action steps

Ask your manager or members of the change management team the following questions:

- What are the benefits and business reasons for the change?

- What is happening inside the business or external to the business that is creating the need to change?

- How do these external or internal drivers impact the business, our organization, our department, and me as an employee?

- What do our customers want or expect that is creating a need for change?

- What are our competitors doing that is creating a need for change?

- What will happen if a change is not made?

- How will the change take place and what will the desired state look like?

- What can I expect to happen and when?

Step 2: Desire action steps

> ## To know what steps to take,
> ## first determine which group you are in:

Group 1:

You are motivated to change simply by understanding what is happening to the business (i.e., what was discussed in the awareness step). You need very little, if any, incentive beyond this basic knowledge. You would be a willing participant and active supporter of the change if allowed.

Group 2:

You are neutral or cautious about the change. You may need incentives, personal attention or definitive consequences for supporting or not supporting the change. You will need to understand how the change will impact you personally (what is in it for you). You will need to understand the risk to the organization and yourself if a change is not made.

Group 3:

You will not support the change no matter what is done. You will either openly obstruct the effort or leave the company. You may be a passive observer but behind the scenes you actively campaign against the change.

If you are in Group 1:

Already supportive of the change.

- Help deploy the change.

- Participate on extended teams to support detailed design activities.

- Help develop training or help test new systems and tools.

- Act as a mentor and coach to other employees.

If you are in Group 2:

Unsure about the change.

- Be patient. You may need time to sort out the change and the impact on you. Continually seek information on the business needs and changing environment. Learn the risks to the business if a change is not made. Determine how the change will impact you personally.

- Have direct communications with a coach or supervisor that understands the change and can communicate the business reasons behind it, as well as the impact on you.

- Voice your objections to the change and understand either why those objections cannot be satisfied, or help the design team modify the solution to account for these objections.

- Understand the personal consequences of not changing, and talk candidly with your supervisor about your choices.

If you are in Group 3:
Outright opposed to the change.

If you chose Group 3, you should talk to your supervisor to understand the consequences of that decision. Determine if you are possibly in Group 2 and just need your concerns listened to and addressed.

Alternatively, this may be the time to explore other work opportunities. Finding work that fits your personal and professional development goals is a critical step for individuals involved in major change initiatives, especially when the direction of the organization is different than the goals of an individual.

Step 3: Knowledge action steps

Seek information from your manager or the change management team about training and educational opportunities. Attend meetings and presentations about the change. Be active in asking questions and seeking out more information.

You should actively pursue the following information during the change process:

1. Clear definition of the change.

2. Education and training opportunities.

3. Information about how the change will impact you.

4. New performance measures.

Knowledge action steps continued

1. *Clear definition of the change.* Each element of the change, including new business processes, new technology or tools, organizational impacts, and changes in job roles should be clearly defined and explained. However, be patient. For some changes, these take time to develop.

2. *Education and training.* Training programs or information should be available for each area of the change, including how to use new systems, tools and business processes. Again, be patient. Much of the information and training will be developed along with the change.

Knowledge action steps continued

3. *How the change will impact you.* Seek out information that explains how the change will impact you and what is expected from you, including:

"How will this change impact my work?"

"What will change for me on a daily basis?"

"What new skills or knowledge do I need?"

4. *New performance measures.* New measures and expectations for performance should be clearly defined and communicated to everyone.

Step 4: Ability action steps

Change is a process. Developing the ability to change means adopting new habits and learning new skills. This takes time. Simply attending training courses is not enough. You will need ongoing support mechanisms and coaching.

In the changed environment, you will encounter circumstances that don't match what you learned in training. In these situations you may be tempted to revert to "the old way of doing things" because of the uncertainty of change.

Instead, raise the issue to your supervisor or change management team and help work through problems with the new design.

Continually work to develop the new skills and behaviors that are required to support the change. When gaps persist, seek additional training to close these gaps.

Ability action steps continued

You can use various methods to build new skills and behaviors:

Monitor your own performance and check yourself against the objectives of the change. Seek help when they don't match. Write down your own goals and take steps to achieve those objectives.

Attend ongoing training and educational programs in areas where you have skill gaps.

Be patient. It takes time to develop new habits and learn new ways of doing work. Be persistent, positive and results-oriented.

Step 5: Reinforcement

Reinforcing the change is just as important as implementing it. Our natural tendency is to revert to the "old ways" of doing things. Every individual plays a role in reinforcing the new way of doing work.

Seek support from your supervisor when the process does not work correctly. Help solve the problems that arise while using new tools and processes. Avoid using old processes when the new processes are not working. Raise issues and make sure they are escalated quickly to the right people.

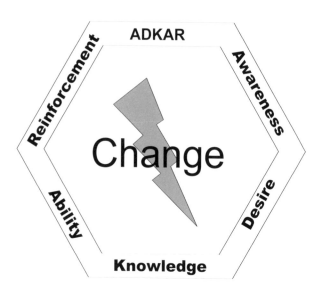

Change opens new doors and new opportunities for both you and the organization. You can take advantage of change to develop professionally and move forward in the organization.

Every business is undergoing change. It is part of today's workplace. Learning how to survive and thrive in a changing environment is a critical skill for advancement and growth.

No change comes without some pain. Certainly, the goal is to minimize that pain and implement the change as quickly as possible. More importantly, you can thrive in a changing environment by using the ADKAR model as a practical tool to understand and manage change.

Notes

Part 3:
Highlights and Tips

Gaining perspective on change

This section provides highlights and puts in perspective topics covered to this point. Also provided are tips for using the tools with your group or department. The purpose of this section is to provide a quick review of the key concepts and suggest ways you can take positive steps to manage the change process.

Change starts from the outside

Nearly all fundamental change taking place within an organization is a response to external stimulus from customers, competitors or market conditions. In most cases financial performance, or the lack thereof, is a critical driver of these changes.

Risk of not changing

Organizations that do not respond to marketplace changes risk customer dissatisfaction, declining market share and poor financial performance. This can apply to both public- and private-sector organizations. The viability of the organization is at risk, as well as the jobs of executives and front-line employees.

What's the hurry?

Typically too much time elapses between the time the organization feels the pain of outside market influences and the time that change initiatives reach front-line managers and employees. The result is that change is needed yesterday. Meetings and more meetings can become the norm as the organization reacts to change.

You have choices

At each step of the change process, you have choices you make that impact your role and how others perceive you. Each of these decisions has consequences, which in many cases you can predict ahead of time. Every conversation we have, whether in meetings or around the coffee pot, reflect our choices about change.

Choices and accountability

Change can be traumatic for everyone involved, even when the final result may be positive. In the end, each person must choose whether they will change or remain the same. We are each accountable for our choices and actions related to change. Adopting this frame of mind will help prevent you from becoming a victim of change.

Taking control of change

You can take control of the change process and how that process impacts you personally and professionally. The ADKAR model provides a concrete action plan for assessing where you are in the change process, which steps you can take to fill in the missing puzzle pieces, and how you can move ahead.

Tips for group activities

The worksheets provided with the ADKAR model are effective to use with groups or teams. They can stimulate conversation and provide a basis for discussion that will help your team navigate the change process.

Group activities

Team size fewer than six

For groups with fewer than six members, complete each of the worksheets in the ADKAR model for the change occurring in your organization as individuals first. Bring your final score sheet to your group meeting.

As a group, complete the worksheets using an easel (flip chart). In this process, you should repeat the same process you used individually, but use the collective input from the group. Then create a group score card.

Now compare your personal scores with the group scores. Discuss among your group why any differences or similarities exist with how you rated each area of the ADKAR model. Create an action plan for each person and for the group as a whole.

Team size six or more

By following these steps, teams of six or more can facilitate a large group session with great results.

1. Have members of the group complete the worksheets on their own.

2. Bring together the entire team, and divide the group into smaller teams of two or three members each. Avoid having groups with more than four members per team.

3. Have each sub-team break out into separate rooms or separate areas of a larger room, and using an easel (flip chart), complete each ADKAR worksheet.

4. Once complete (about 45 minutes), bring the teams back together and allow each team to present the highlights of each area of the ADKAR model.

5. Compare the scores from the final score sheets of each team, and identify patterns and themes for each area.

Be sure to designate someone to take notes and document the findings of the group meeting. Assign a group of volunteers to create an action plan.

Remember that everyone has a role in the change process.

Part 4:
For employees who are part of change management teams

Research results

Team structure

What are the top criteria for a good change management team member?

1. Knowledgeable about the business and enthusiastic about the change.

2. Excellent communications skills; willing to listen and share.

3. Total commitment to the project, the process and the results.

4. Ability to remain open-minded and visionary.

5. Respected within the organization as an apolitical catalyst for strategic change.

"a passion for the vision"

"willing and able to participate fully in change management"

"resilient enough to succeed in uphill challenges"

Planning

What activities did successful change management teams do during the planning phase of the project?

- Interview sponsors to understand project goals and scope.

- Educate and train the team on change management and change strategies.

- Educate top managers on how to be successful project sponsors; establish a project steering committee.

- Develop a communication plan addressing all levels to be impacted by the project.

Planning steps continued

- Validate the need for change and the subsequent benefits and consequences.

- Charter a change management team and develop a change management plan.

- Collect background research and benchmarking information to validate needs and benefits of effectively managing the change.

- Begin early communications about why the change is happening.

- Identify potential barriers and begin activities to address these barriers.

Design

What activities did successful change management teams do during the design phase of the project?

- Implement the communication plan; provide a continuous source of information to all employees, which includes the reason for the change, benefits of the change, a timeline, progress status and goals.

- Ensure that input is collected from all parts of the organization; create feedback channels for employees and managers on a constant basis.

- Secure commitment and support from all management levels by presenting the project as a priority of the organization.

Design steps continued

- Identify barriers to the change and the root causes of those barriers; establish plans to reduce resistance, including a change readiness assessment.

- Begin to share elements of the design with the organization.

- Help top-management sponsors stay involved in the process; help them understand their role as project sponsors.

Implementation

What activities did successful change management teams do during the implementation phase?

- Communicate to all employees at all levels; use different overviews for different audiences; repeat the message.

- Provide training, education and information to all impacted employees; maintain a rapid, focused pace of learning and implementation so enthusiasm is not lost.

- Recognize the project as a priority and the design team as a knowledge-sharing authority within the organization; foster support for the change and its developers.

Implementation steps continued

- Establish channels so that employees can provide feedback (anonymously or publicly) to the implementation team.

- Help top-management sponsors execute their responsibilities; encourage them to remain visible and maximize direct interaction with employees.

- Recognize the accomplishments of all participants; develop measures for success and post progress charts and timelines where everyone can see them.

Communications

How often should you communicate information about your change?

In nearly all cases, teams would have communicated with employees more frequently than they actually did on their project. Over 85% of teams recommended communications at least weekly (see figure below).

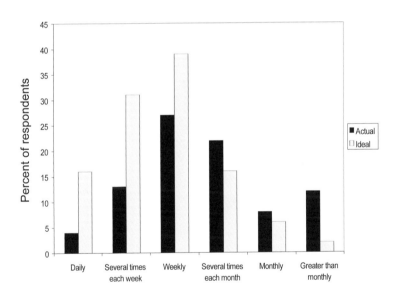

Communications frequency

Communications

What communication methods did your team use and what methods were most effective?

Teams listed a variety of media and other methods they found helpful in keeping communication channels open. The most effective communication methods were:

- Face-to-face communication (both one-on-one and group meetings).

- Email updates and announcements.

- Regular meetings (formal and informal).

- CEO or senior-management presentations.

**Most effective communication media
used by participants**

One-on-one conversation

Meetings and presentations

Email

Voice mail and conference calls

Weekly magazine

Workshops/training sessions

Video/inter-company TV broadcast

Posters/charts

Focus groups

Intranet web page

Memos

Informal cross-company dialogue

Organization-wide announcements

Newsletters

Media types used by teams

Training

What were the most important elements of your training plan?

- Identified the competencies and performance levels required by the change.

- Assessed gaps between current and desired competencies to customize training.

- Scheduled training carefully to match actual implementation (timing was good); coordinated with project management.

- Provided time for all to attend training.

- Tied training to end goal by defining expected outcomes.

- Conducted workshops with mock work scenarios.

- Clearly identified the practical application of the training.

- Trained all managers.

Training steps continued

- Provided education in both technical skills and interpersonal/change management skills in order to institutionalize the change in managers and staff.

- Reinforced the need for change.

- Established performance level standards.

- Evaluated the training.

- Emphasized train-the-trainer to speed up knowledge-transfer process.

- Trained operational managers to conduct training in their areas.

- Had parts of the training led by sponsors.

- Used instructional designers to create training.

- Provided hands-on exercises in the training.

- Obtained user input in process walk-through.

- Tailored system training for specific user.

References

Best Practices in Change Management. Prosci Research, 2000.
Prosci's Best Practices in Change Management *benchmarking study combined findings over a two-year period from 254 organizations from 40 countries and six continents. The objective of the study was to uncover best practices for managing the human side of change and for creating great executive sponsorship.*

Perfect Change, The. Prosci Research, 2000.
Research in change management and business process design with more than 700 companies over a four-year period shows that successful change can be modeled and repeated. By using the ADKAR model first introduced in The Perfect Change, *you can increase the likelihood that your change will be a success.*

Business Process Reengineering Best Practices. Prosci Research, 1999.
248 companies shared lessons learned from their business process reengineering projects.

Prosci Research Publications

- ❏ *Project Planning Toolkit*
- ❏ *Reengineering Design Toolkit*
- ❏ *Business Case Toolkit*
- ❏ *Change Management Toolkit*
- ❏ *Complete Reengineering Toolkit Set*
- ❏ *Business Process Reengineering Best Practices Report*
- ❏ *Business Process Reengineering Best Practices Report with Future Role of IT*
- ❏ *Managing Change Best Practices Report*
- ❏ *The Perfect Change*
- ❏ *The Change Management Series*
- ❏ *Employee's Survival Guide to Change*
- ❏ *Innovative Practices in Human Resources*
- ❏ *Call Center Best Practices — Special Operations Edition*
- ❏ *Call Center Best Practices— Special Technology Edition*
- ❏ *Call Center Measurement Toolkit*

Contact information

Prosci Research
(970) 203-9332
Fax: (970) 669-7005
email: prosci@prosci.com
Toll free - (800) 700-2831

Manager's Edition now available

For managers working to implement organizational change.

Prosci announces the Manager's Edition to the *Employee's Survival Guide to Change*. This special edition includes:

- teambuilding exercises
- benchmarking data for change initiatives
- worksheets for large or small groups

Learn to deal with the human side of organizational change.

The Manager's Edition is designed to help you prepare yourself and your employees for the upcoming change.

For more information, call (800) 700-2831 or (970) 203-9332 when dialing internationally.